# WESTPORT
## POINT ★ Poems

## Also by Richard Dey

Poetry

*Bequia Poems*

*Selected Bequia Poems*

*The Loss of the Schooner* Kestrel *& Other Poems*

Nonfiction

*Adventures in the Trade Wind*
The Story of Morris Nicholson, Pioneer Charterboat Skipper,
and of Yacht Chartering in the West Indies
in the Half Century after the Second World War

*In the Way of Adventure*
John Caldwell and Palm Island
(a chapbook)

Editor

*The Schooner* Pilgrim's *Progress*
A Voyage around the World 1932–1934
Donald C. Starr

# WESTPORT POINT ★ Poems

## Richard Dey

Offshore Press
Boston 2017

Copyright © 2017 by Richard Dey.

First Edition

ISBN:  Softcover    978-1-5434-2069-2
       eBook        978-1-5434-2068-5

All rights reserved. This book or any portion thereof may not be reproduced or used in any manner whatsoever without the express written permission of the publisher except for the use of brief quotations in a book review or scholarly journal.

Print information available on the last page.

Published by Offshore Press. rdeyop@gmail.com

Rev. date: 05/19/2017

❦

OFFSHORE PRESS
Boston

for my sons and grandchildren

# Contents

Houseboat, a Prelude / 1

## I  FISHING
Outside the Steamer Lanes / 5
WIND AGAINST THE TIDE / 7
    Fog / 7
    Wind Against the Tide / 9
    "The Devil's Pocket Hole" / 12
    Boulder Heights / 13
    China Royal Restaurant / 14
Swordfishing / 15
In the Eye of the Swordfish / 16
Offshore Warbler / 18
The Loss of the *Navigator* / 19
Andy's, in Winter / 21
Requiem for a Shrimp Boat / 22

## II  *FRANGIPANI* POEMS
    The Launching / 27
    In an Eddy / 28
    At Anchor / 29
    Capsized! / 30
    In Fog / 31
    On Her Mooring / 32
    Paddling Home / 33
    Hauling Her Out / 35
    Taking out the Mooring / 36
    In a Shed / 37

## III  LETTER FROM WESTPORT POINT

## IV  WHAT IT WAS
Dinghies at a Dock / 47
Swamped / 48
Beetle Cat Race, Labor Day / 49
What It Was / 50
How Like a Painting / 51

Elegy in a Seaside Town / 52
East of the Bell / 53
Lines on a Dinghy / 54
Luck of the Strike / 55
North Wind Blowing / 57

**V  MOORING SPARS**
Sailor at a Sawbuck / 61
To My Son, Fourteen Months Old, in the Nuclear Age / 63
Mishaum Blues / 64
The Relic / 65
Tonging / 67
Gleam, Vanishing Saltmarsh / 68
The Uninsured / 69
The Broadbills / 70
A Waiting Game / 72
Under Poncho / 74
Elegy Sketched in an Estuary Cove / 76
Arrival, Westport Point / 77
Mooring Spars / 78

Acknowledgements / 81

There are those to whom place is unimportant,
But this place, where sea and fresh water meet,
Is important—
    —Theodore Roethke, "The Rose"

## Houseboat, a Prelude

It's on the one not at a dock or out
on a mooring but moored near
the Harpoon Bar, amongst the cordgrasses
across the channel from the work boats
tied up at the town wharf
                                that I live

You're most likely to find the *Hibiscus Inn*
not at high tide when she's inconspicuous
(or, at least, not an eyesore)
but when the tide's out and she's hard aground
her stern high and dry in the marsh mud

and anything not secure is falling—
loss out of the corners like marbles
love like the flag whose halyard comes uncleated
courage off the fiddled table top like a cocktail glass
pride like fresh baked bread awash in the scuppers

It's then, assuming some foothold,
some grasp amidst the disruption
and despite the chance of a place ashore
that I make my passages in her
and write these poems
                                Welcome aboard

# I
# FISHING

## Outside the Steamer Lanes

Like kids beneath the Big Top, open-eyed
and half-afraid, we'd been expecting them.
We lay along the edge of the canyoned shelf
in ninety fathoms, outside the steamer lanes,
where you can see the continent end on
the sounder whose graph jig-jags in sudden fall.
A swell was running, obscuring the horizon.
We four stood hauling the last set of traps
beside the hauler whose hydraulic winch
sang up the fathoms of polypropylene;
we stood there tired enough to feel at one
with the sea we'd danced on, not lifting a boot,
as the pots came up, trawl after long trawl.
The words we spoke were few—drum beats to mark
the rhythm of our work: swinging the pots
inboard and landing them to cull their catch
of clamp-clawed lobster and crab. Then we rebaited
and dragged each one across the afterdeck,
ready to fish again. The pots set quickly;
you have to watch the trawl line joining them
to see no loop ensnares an arm or leg.

It grew pitch-black and we forgot about them.
Three floodlights bathed the sea around us in
a ring of light. No running lights shone but ours.
When the last pot swung dripping off the boom,
lucent with lobsters and with hake, they came—
long, lithe, white-bellied, turning and unturning,
all teeth and muscle, not on film, to fin
the water white for dead hake and bleeding claws,
four or five of them, each one coffin-sized.
We took her out of gear. The diesel idled.
I watched while Russell, beside the bulwark, harpooned
one for the hell of it, without a lily.
Spooked, the fish pulled free of the shank and sounded.

"Jus' practicin'," he said and gave a shrug
and turned from the sea whose waters were our living.
The trawl was done. Richie brought the boat
around and we steamed inshore, sharks in our wake.

# Wind Against the Tide

Like some wines our love could neither mature nor travel.
—Graham Greene, *The Comedians*

**Fog**


It was early fall or late summer,
I don't know which,
but the lobstering was good.
Home from the sea,
I found no one and the fog coming in:
no note, nothing except the fog.
I showered, opened a Heineken,
and watched the fog roll in the harbor,
fog thick as cavalry
cantering across a plain,
its silence full of thundering hooves.

                  As I stood waiting,
the fog seemed to steepen into waves,
marshaled in long fetches, deep troughs.
The fieldlawns before me swelled
like Nantucket Shoals.
Soon its grayness thickened into legend,
dripping hushed and huge
off the window screens,
weighing on branches like sodden snowfall.
I was waiting, Slim, for you.

Angels descended over the house, circling.
They had black wings and choired
in the thick black tongue of the fog.
I heard the horn of some passing ...
I saw fog, like beads of sweat,
on the fieldstone walls.

On the southwest breeze,
I smelled honeysuckle fresh as first love.

At last, into the fog, I hurled a lamp.

## Wind Against the Tide

River gray and uninviting this morning.
Wind northwest. Tide falling.
                        Look:
You can see whitecaps, yachts hard-pressed
and pulling hard on their moorings,
the channel buoys too, marsh flats
like islands in some archipelago ...

This morning I woke with you
and remembered the landfall years
that saw us, toward their end, exchange
the Charles for the Acoaxet River,
Frost Street off Mass Ave for this
estuary peninsula and a harbor
we thought we both could use.

Gray betrays your brown hair now, and I'm ...
I'd hate to wake up without this river's view.

You look nice this morning, really.
"Thank you."
            You're smiling,
reserved: Why the tears?

The sense of the tide
falling against the wind
is killing me too.
                Look:
There goes a fishboat
into the spray hurled up against it,
probably to New Bedford for ice.

It's hard to know what to make
of those incoming years in
the Cambridge that was
our Paris, of the inside city years when

we saved to have hot pastrami
sandwiches at the Wursthaus,
were untroubled by used cars.
We were each other's only public then,
our only confidence was in
what the other said. So confident
were we,
            we never married.

You'd just begun to study archaeology
("the fine art of digging," you called it),
and I was beginning to write
with my offshore view. Thank God
we had no children, have nothing
of material value.
                We did
have the sense, then, of exploration
and discovery, of sharing in
a kind of adventure, didn't we?
At least we can say that.
Those were hard years though,
        clawing to windward.

"But we always had good bread."
Aroma of bread freshly baked.
"They were good years, but
they couldn't go on forever."
                           What
is the river doing with us?
What each of us lived for then
is coming true, but not for us.

Wind northwest. Most of the pots
are offshore now. Look: The clouds
are continental, gray.
                    I doubt the boat
will go out tonight,
not that it matters much, any more.

Fishing's no life for love.
Have you your books?

"We've hurt each other too much
to go on together, I think."

"Did I tell you about the turtle handles
on the pots in St. Vincent?
What they're thought to ..."
"Don't drink today, OK?"

River gray and uninviting. Wind northwest.
What are these words now, Slim,
but wind against the tide?

Have a nice day.

## "The Devil's Pocket Hole"

Shrouded by fog, wave-lashed,
a wreck lies not long on the beach.
It would be hard to say
what she was or to know how
she took the seas—except,
in the end, badly.

This beach has been good to me.
I prefer palms along an emerald bay but
in bleak scenes are sometimes others.
Away from the oak frames I shoulder
into the westerly winds, hoping
for a different sight, a sail
would be fine, upon
the sea that does not care what
it takes from you or gives.

Once around the end
of this beach, barrier to what
by a British admiral was called
"the devil's pocket hole," you see
the harbor and fields plowed brown,
the wooded shores; and there,
on the estuary point, the house.
Is it whose frames are fitted
to ride out hurricanes, stronger
than we who have lived
so far from it and apart,
so faithlessly?          I used to like it here
in sight of the winds that march across
the marsh grass, in the absence of fog,
before the wreck was ours. "Take heart, boy,
in the sudden rising
of the white egret," the wind
of course is not saying, "in the wing
song of such long standing."

## Boulder Heights

Here, where the winds are muted by the firs
and the air above these cumulous clouds is thin,
everywhere it's sharp ascent, steep fall.
To the west is a mountain summit where the snowcap
shines year-round. My sister, who asks after you,
tells me lions roam its north slope.

Tonight, to the eastward and far below,
beyond the lower ridge lines,
I see the city lights spangled on the plain.
They look like harbor lights seen from a deck offshore.

We were happy once down in a city like that—
off Saturday mornings with our backpacks to Haymarket
and the "Hey, hey, *ho* for a dollah!"
of the hawkers hawking their oranges
and asparagus in Boston's North End—
happy in the foreign setting of an open market.
I don't know why we'll never call a place
geologic as this one "home."

But why—What roar is that I'm hearing?—
*why* is the wrong question about a love
that was more like the sea than these mountains;

why only hauls back, brings up
starfish, monkfish, rock
in the scalloper's dredge.

## China Royal Restaurant

The wonton soup was good.

It's good we see each other
infrequently, but often enough,
that we can talk: You've found
the oldest ceramic kiln in Central America,
and now are writing your Masters—
I feel part of the discovery, oddly ...
         that we
can talk (with a northeaster swaying
the traffic lights outside and the boat
with double spring lines at dock)
as we always have.
        I've always liked
something about this setting,
and not just that it brings to mind Conrad
in the South China Sea, Malraux
in Shanghai, or H. M. Tomlinson
in Singapore ... I like the strangeness,
I suppose. What better place to recall
a warm spring rain that night
after a bike-ride wheeling north
through Harvard Square?
         This pagoda
suits my enduring love for you, Slim,
now a love without desire.

And *that,* of the many places
strange to this Yankee sailor,
is the strangest port of call.

## Swordfishing

*Nada.* The *Quest* had been ten days at sea with nothin' doing—
not a single fish—and all we wanted was "a trip."
This was in the time of fireflies—prime for swordfishing
up on the banks. Where were the birds above the rich tiderip?

Full swells swallowed the pulpit, normally in summer fishboats
an easy chair; it was so rough we had no spotter planes.
No yachtsmen out for a cruise, we crew were at each other's
    throats
and cursed from masthead hoops, where we stood scanning for
    tell-tail fins.

Then, at four in the afternoon, they horned-up big and unfazed—
incredibly enough, a school of them, chocolate and blue.
Curt, broad-shouldered, out on the pulpit, got really crazed:
In two hours, he harpooned twenty-four fish, missing two.

I fed him lily and bib lines, one set after the next, and watched
the tide balls scatter toward the sea rim, every which-way.
By midnight, we had boated twenty-one and stood amazed
by business in these tiderip waters, the trip's lasting pay.

## In the Eye of the Swordfish

> ... my fellow citizen of the sea, *Xiphias gladius* ...
> —Ernest Hemingway, "Cuban Fishing"

The ironed fish, entangled in line,
resurfaced and turning toward the boat
in blind revenge, swam dead ahead,
its terrible eyes beautiful, intent.

In furious confusion, rolling
and twisting and crazed, it had wound
the lily line around its girth
as the dart burned, deep by its brain.

Once struck, all swordfish sound and run,
but how they deal with the event
depends on where the dart invades
and individual temperament.

If struck in the chest, by gill or heart,
they can go belly-up in a flash;
others flee as if in exile,
then die, exhausted. Struck in the flesh,

a fish, towing a window weight
and flag attached to the lily line,
can go for hours; others break free,
the dart embedded harmlessly.

Can shock alone account for those
who, like Indians heading for the hills,
dive straight down to drive their broad bills
into the mud, up to their gills?

This one that surfaced, tangled in line,
charged the bow of our wooden boat
and with its power boldly drove
its sword, as if into a throat,

three inches deep. The tip broke off as the fish,
stunned by the jolt, settled, went slack.
To land it, I looped a strap around
its tail, cinching it like a sack.

Hung from a block at davit's end,
and hauled up to the rail and bled,
the colors of its scaleless flesh
turned silver and blue and green—and dead.

The lidless eyes, as big as baseballs,
stared, unmoving and unmoved.
Did it not know us—our wild need
for freedom, food, and being loved?

## Offshore Warbler

Seemingly from out of nowhere,
round as a ping-pong ball and as light,
with a sleepy, fetching, bewildered stare,
yellow-breasted, black-winged, and fair-
ly called "a miracle of flight,"

the warbler lands on deck, inside the rail,
and hops among the traps and roam-
ing traplines, and flies inside the wheel-
house as if this were a swank hotel,
checks in, and makes itself at home.

Storm-blown off its coastal flyway,
it looks us each in the eye.
The bird seems happy with its stay
aboard, unpoisoned by salt spray.
We give it water, a dead fly.

Its eyes reflect an eerie sky
and when the boat returns to shore,
we go our onshore ways. The bird flies
off, over the salt marsh, and I
walk uphill houseward, my gait unsure.

# The Loss of the *Navigator*

As I was walking down the wharf,
    John Borden called out, "Poet!"
He stuffed a bait bag, winked, and scoffed
    at my story. "You think you know it

"all, huh? ' ... the sea has claimed more victims,
    and fishing's a hard profession,
eased somewhat by its air of freedom ...'
    Well, let me clue you in."

I leaned against a stack of traps.
    The scalloper had gone down,
vanished without a trace or contact.
    John's *Julie B* had half-drowned.

"Overloaded with scallop bags
    lashed to the rails, top-heavy,
she ran into in a barrier sea
    and flipped," he said, "like a Chevy."

I'd pictured scallops packed to her beams
    and heavier than her ballast,
pressing her open along her seams.
    "What about the crew?" I asked.

"Captain Mike, the Mate, Duvol,
    the engineer and deckhands,
were down below, out of the gale,
    dreaming of foreign lands,

"no doubt, surrounded by their fortune."
    He cracked his wise-guy smile.
"They lived as long as the air held out,
    which wasn't a long while.

"Mike should've steamed home. He'd gotten his trip,
    wouldn't you say? But, *No*.
He had to stay another day,
    make another tow."

"But she was an older boat ..." "Old, right:
    'No mortgage payment,' read."
"Still, it seems a mystery..."
    "... like hell. It was greed."

## Andy's, in Winter

A fisherman's blue
knit cap on
top of a red vinyl bar
stool, and his salt-stiff
gloves on the brown
Formica bar, next to three
ones and a five.

Jukebox unplugged.
Bar out of bourbon.

The fisherman, a small
man with a loud
shrill laugh, poised over
the Captain Fantastic
pinball machine with
his draft beer, waiting

for the right
woman, a break in
the weather. Getting
a phone call. The door nailed
down by blowy cold.

No baseball on TV.
Fred Lynn in Florida.

Out the picture window lights
of a tanker in
ballast, bound
to the south'ard, cutting
across the icy bay.

At the fisherman's side,
a sheathed knife.

# Requiem for a Shrimp Boat

    For Paul Brayton, Richard Earle, Alex Leonard,
        Grant Moore, & Russell Walters

The shrimp boat, bought cheap, and brought north from the Gulf
for lobstering in the North Atlantic had grown
so old and so neglected she couldn't get
insured (and, anyways, the heyday for
offshore lobstering was over), so Bud,
after getting permission from the EPA,
scuttled her: took everything off her
of any value, which wasn't a whole lot,
pulled the fuel tanks and drained the engine oils,
poured two truckloads of cement into her fish-hold,
and towed her out to a spot off Pierson's Ledge.
*Sea Queen* was the one the congressman went
aboard that time: Bud was the port's highliner,
and it was his gear that got torn up by
the foreign trawlers, and the congressman—
What was his name?—was up for reelection
and looking for local coverage, I suppose.
Anyways, Sweetpea took the chainsaw down
into the forepeak and *zip-zip-ziiiiip-zip,*
just like that, he cut a four-foot chunk
out of her stem, right at the waterline,
and somebody else opened all the seacocks.
This was in May, when the sea was calm as a millpond.
No one said much of anything as we watched
her go—she tilted forward, rolled and settled—
though Bud, for once, passed around a bottle;
it was, you could say, very businesslike.

We'd handled thousands and thousands of pounds of lobsters
every trip, and seen them blue and albino,
and others blue and white, or brown and white—
calicoes beautiful as watercolors;
and we'd seen some thirty-pounders (we had to tape

their claws), the heavy barnacled veterans of
one hundred fifty years on the bottom, or more.

But in my dreams what I see are the shorts
squirming and crackling and shining, all piled-up
in wire baskets lined-up ten and fifteen deep,
outside the deckhouse. Their molted, mottled shells
would dry to a flat sheen, dull as a stone's;
and then, as you were hauling pot after pot
(we fished twelve hundred traps on thirty trawls),
you'd smell them cooking in the galley, see
the steam escape out deckhouse windows like souls.
At night, on watch, I'd have my basket's worth:
the back, with one good squeeze of the palm, cracked down
the center. We seldom bothered with the claws.
It took a lot of little bugs to make
a pound of lobster meat. The meat was stuffed
in Ziploc bags and put down on the ice
in the hold way aft of the rope spools and spare gear—
even buried, some trips, deep in the ice.

After we'd unloaded the catch and made sure
the warden wasn't around, we'd bring up the meat
and then one of us was on the highway north
at daybreak, driving to a restaurant
just off the Commons. It was there, inside
the walk-in fridge, while dealing with the man
in his tuxedo, that I, myself, sometimes felt
a little trapped. The meat tasted the same
as meat from any lobster. It was used
in salads, I suppose, or lobster rolls.
To us it was cash: "Bug Gold," we called it.
Of course, this was before that law got passed
saying all pots must have escape vents for
the sexually immature.
      The old
queen sank in ten minutes, in sixty fathoms,
right about where, come fall and the cooler water,
we used to find the lobsters thick as gumdrops.
They were that way once right along the shore—

wade into a tide pool and pluck out a meal,
was how it was for my great-grandparents
and, before them, the animals and Indians.
"Gotta make that hay while the sun shines,"
Bud used to say. He's off the Carolinas
in a new boat, fishing for some kind of
exotic crab, I hear. Me? I'm just
as glad not to be offshore all the time,
hauling and picking, baiting and stacking and setting,
trawl after trawl. And sites are hard to find.
There just are not as many boats out there
and those that are, are steel, with big overheads;
they're fishing more and more pots on longer trips—
all for fewer and fewer bugs. Of course,
the price keeps going up. It always does.

## II
## *FRANGIPANI* POEMS

SAILORS TRADITIONALLY TALK to their boats, referring to and addressing them as women, and seeing in them certain human attributes. The beginnings of this anthropomorphism are lost in time. It seems likely, however, that the beauty and behavior of boats afloat, along with the fact that sailors have mostly been men, and men without women for long periods of time, accounts for this. The practice persists today. *Frangipani* is a 13-foot Beetle Cat, wooden and bronze fastened. Launched in 1983, she was one of the last built in Padanaram by Leo Telesmanick.

**The Launching**

Do not be deceived by the calm
high waters you slip spanking into,
nor by these ceremonial attentions.
The history of ships runs hard
with trial, easy with whim.
This coin, placed in your mast step,
is nailed there for luck. No one
can say what, in its give
and take, the tide will do. We know
only the sound of waters rushing
parted past your bows,
that even as it takes you,
you must take the tide. Is that
the wind? Answer and go.

**In an Eddy**

This is smart sailing, using
the eddy to our advantage,
isn't it? Sailing the edge of
the channel, we take the eddy's
swift countertide and go
some distance, or poke
the bows briefly into it
to keep from being swept
away. This eddy sailing's
a local knowledge held close
to the heart. It's almost magical
to those not in the know,
who see us glide against
the logic of buoys leaning
and go faster, often, than
wind could ever drive us.

But even on the windy bright
days, an eddy's only good
for so long. Sooner or later
the tide will have its way.
And while it lets us go some
places freely, an eddy, with
its grip and whorl, keeps us
close-in by these shell-strewn,
rocky shallows and reminds me,
as if this were like loving,
how close we sometimes are,
*Frangipani,* to smashed stems.

## At Anchor

You, no doubt, would rather be
tacking and jibing, flirting with
the rush of wind and kicking up
your white heels again, strutting your stuff—

but there are times, *Frangipani,*
when all our sailing seems to come
to this swinging alone on plenty of scope
in a protected lee; when the sun

overhead and the breeze are warm,
and the osprey's banking wing is more
arresting than the trim of sail;
when the horizon holds no claim.

## Capsized!

The autumn day was fair, the wind nor'west,
the tide high & falling, and we—the boat
and I—were tacking smartly across the channel,
north toward home, when the gust struck.
It was like other gusts—you could see it coming—
it did not look like a gleam in Neptune's eye.
The boat was beamy, stiff, a stable platform,
and I was hiked out way to windward, sure
of my sense for the wind's weight, the hull's hold.
To spill the wind I did not slack the sheet
until—up, up, and O-*VER*—it was too late
and there to leeward, was my pride awash
in a Hell's tangle of lines & spars & cloth,
and the boat disgusted, saying "I told you so!"

**In Fog**

I know the sun's up there and not
that cold white disc only, knifing
in and out of the fog, ghostly.
I know there are real islands out
beyond these mud flats looking like islands,
that the air is clear, unremarked
by these groaning horns, damn clanging gongs.
I should have been an astronaut.

This fog is too much like that other
fog with its thick gray isolation,
its backward looking, unlifting shutdown.
And I thought we were clear of the land—
that love, like the wind, brought clarity.
We're hard aground. Which way's the tide?

**On Her Mooring**

How does she fare in the pull
and swing of her tethered dancing? Might she break free?
Does the line chafe badly in its chock,
could the mooring drag?
And does the wind banter in her rigging,
the rush of current deride her painted hull?
Is there someone aboard, stealing her?
Or does she raise the sail herself,
take the darkened water as
a wild duck takes the September sky?

It's ten o'clock and I close a book of stories
set in Berlin; am, in a disturbed way,
not unsatisfied. And turning out the light,
I listen to the damp wind sing darkly at my window.
Should I row out to her, my demimonde,
check that she's all right? License,
nor bill of sale, nor premiums paid,
insure possession—not of anything or one.
All I know is where we've been.

**Paddling Home**

It's not supposed to be this way, of course.
You figure home by five before the wind
lets go, the gnats arrive. But you sailed further than
you'd planned & now it's late, the tide outgoing.

At first you managed in the dying air
by shifting your weight & shifting without motion,
keeping a lee bow, staying outside
the wind shadow, working the eddies.
You skimmed the squiggle with an inch to spare

only to find, and with the mooring in sight,
the wind had died. *Died.* Not a breath of air.
You were becalmed, fit to be tied. And thirsty!
The boat was going *backwards*. Anchoring
would get you nowhere. What to do?

Not for nothing do you store a paddle.
But paddling a sailboat is like pushing
a Lincoln Continental out of gas,
your shoulder to the door frame & hand on the wheel.
You huff & puff & curse but don't give up,
fueled by what you saw, or thought you knew:

not Paradise Island but a New Atlantis
looming in the haze like Vegas in
the desert or Dubai on shifting sands,
immortal on the Mid-Atlantic Ridge;
where along wide palm-lined avenues
fragrant with frangipani Trade Wind swept,
rise skyscrapers of luminous design,
each balcony a garden turning with
the sun & gardeners,
      the men & women
in their dark moods & bright, turning with them,
one with the surrounding land & sea;
where poets stand among the senators,

brokering bills for beauty & transcendence,
and there is wealth for all & love without
borders, & a T-wharf hosting spaceships ...

Even now, paddling for all you're worth,
salt stings your eyes, blinking with Atlantis.
But on the porch you'll drink with friends and laugh
and say, *Oh, it was just one of those days.*

## Hauling Her Out

I thought I'd lost you off Southard's Point until
I let the peak halyard go and scandalized
the main. What wind! And just our luck to have
it drive your bows nearly under the tide
running contrary to the wind, its salt
spray stinging and bitter cold. I could breathe in
the woodsmoke, though, see the trailer on
the asphalt ramp; I'd heard its black clattering.

This cotter pin confounds me every time,
as if you were afraid to face the shed;
but think of it as one long summer's night
you're sailing into, an evening out on the pale
sea sparkling with phosphorescence. Be grateful
you get this time out of the wind and tide.

## Taking out the Mooring

    For Chip Gillespie


It was a cold, late November day
and I was catching my breath, standing
on the shore, surrounded by
heavy limp chain, snarls of line,
and frozen shackles, the anchor
heavy and loose in the dinghy, flukes canted—
all of it dripping eel grass, mud-covered,
and looking like bones in an X-ray—

when a loon's call came high out of the marsh,
downwind, over me. I looked out
toward where the boat and orange tide ball
had been and saw nothing
but her absence and mine from this earth,
and the wind on the water like breath.

## In a Shed

Hard to see you, *Frangipani,*
in this dim, earthen light
saw-horsed like lumber to the drafts
thieving through cracks in the siding;
in this damp skylessness
smelling faintly of turpentine
and dry eel grass, hard to know why
I've pulled back the heavy, snow-drifted doors,
what I'm doing here myself,
talking through clouds of breath ...
Listen: this winter gale
is neither to your liking or mine;
but isn't the tide, beneath
cracked ice, running over the Lion's Tongue?

# III
# LETTER FROM WESTPORT POINT

# Letter from Westport Point

**I**
You'd think envy all we had in common,
the way we live, traveling back and forth,
needing the sea and city both, nature
not less than culture, life and a life of the mind.
    What's new in the bookstores? Have you been to the theater?
The tide on the river is high, now; the wind
sou'west and gusty, its softness gone and growing
harder; the salt marsh golden and dying, alive
with heron, teal, egret, and cormorant.
I continue sailing *Frangipani*
on afternoons, the sense of exploration,
of going by wind and tide, yet summertime's
beneath the geese wedging this October sky.
The lobster boats, offshore and way to the east'ard,
are hauling ten pounds per pot, which isn't bad.
*Side Show's* scalloping on Nantucket Shoals,
though not with me this fall. My work progresses.
    And did I tell you how another boat,
this one out of Gloucester, went down on Georges Bank?
You have to wonder, or I do, about the men
who go offshore ("It's a living," they'd say),
about the risks they take for landlessness.
Of the *Captain Cosmo,* nothing was found—
no raft, hatch cover, fish box, oil slick, nor body.
She foundered on a clear and child-eyed Saturday.
Boats everywhere, of all kinds, got caught and had
to run with it, so suddenly did the wind
come up, growing in not thirty minutes,
from cat's-paw to the claws of a hungry cat.
    You will not be surprised to hear, I suppose,
that I rode out that early autumn gale
aboard Ed Yeoman's sloop, surfing all
the way from Martha's Vineyard to Nantucket
at knots the gauges could not register.
The little sloop, like the little *Moss* before,

drove sideways leaning while she forward lunged,
every ropeyarn tingling like a wire.
In the raw unexpected light of that wild day,
the seas built quickly, their crested blue waves breaking
and raging white as far as the eye could see.
We aboard Ed's able sloop were lucky
and knew not only what we were doing, but
the fear and pride of it—which is, I'd say,
what it means to have respect for the sea.

      Such moments of authenticity (the phrase
is Heidegger's), when we transcend our every-
dayness, are seldom known, however, even
out of a port like this one. I admit
there is about this rural seaside living
a sense of false content, of peacefulness
not quite real. And in the winter, when a few
stoic starving swans prevail against
the river's ice floes, and everything white yellows,
this place is unspeakable; I leave for Bequia.
Is there no place without its contrary winds?

      It's not, however, as you fear—that I live
in intellectual isolation. The river
affords the freedom to be alone, and speaks
the tidal tongue of change and renewal I find
essential to this solitary craft.
It's a freedom, like others; it has its costs.
The beach is deserted, windswept, and gray; but in
the mind that walks there bloom frangipani.

      No, in your cities I feel fevered slightly
and giddy, on the dodge, not unlike
a swordfish breaching an eighty-pound test line.
Though I miss the air electric with news, fashion,
and your iridescent, peripatetic talk,
though I love the theater, when I'm away all
I want is the road back, to drive fast and feel
the pavement slope to the end of the continent.
I like to reach the Point, downshift and brake;
and then, shutting down the engine, to hear
a fish boat steaming down the river, surfroar

or slapping of halyards, the rivering salt air—
all welcome me to this windward village still
beneath the moving continent of sky.
But I'll be along to see you soon, I hope.

## II
After writing the other day (in the morning
as I always do, or try to), I read
of fifty-four 24 megaton H-bomb tipped
Titan rockets—eighteen of them underground
in silver silos around the old cow town
of Wichita, thirty-six more beneath
the Arizona desert and Arkansas hills.
The silos are designed for one shot only,
the outcome of their trajectory being
but half a world and tide, or a movie away.
    I don't know that it matters, but you see
what I mean, now, by a sense of false content:
of living on the river (the boats are bow-to,
straining against the current), beside the sea
and looking out toward the horizon on
which sails a topsail schooner when, over her,
fly Stratofortresses and under her
cruise submarines that make the whitest shark
seem tame, or at least—considering the state
of haphazardness, of fear and doom and pride
in which we live—at least something on which you
can place an unambiguous, plain emotion.
And that's not to mention the "leasing" of Georges Banks,
the risk of drilling those rich fields for oil.
Can two days of fuel be worth centuries of fish?
Someone's lost his sense of proportion: *us*.
    If there's anything essential to
our living, or as essential as food and warmth,
is it not a sense of belonging somewhere,
*to* something? Or are we fated to transient
roles as unwilling extras on the statesman's set?
I wonder what the teal and dolphin know.
    We speak of well-being and of living well,
but the Wampanoag Indians, who lived

here first, worshipped Kautantouwit,
"the house of the South west God," from which came all
things good and where they'd go in Afterlife.
I have no expectations for Afterlife
(save that my soul, if such exists, finds new
life in a gull, living on Cuttyhunk),
but if this place today were to have a spirit,
an over-dwelling sense of reverence,
of imagination; if I could finger
the gull's white cry or powerful wing above
the tide, I'd call it Kautantouwit.

    Wherever we find it and however accept
its limitations, can we reaffirm
that place is a mirror and not mere vanity,
a reflection of our inward knowing, something
to breakwater the madness of the fearful,
sad conclusions we face about our time?
Or is this rivering salt air, this view
cheap comfort? This estuary peninsula
irrelevant, a poet's fabrication?

    I see by the boats, easy on their moorings,
and the white herons and blue, tall and hungry
on the gleaming mudflats, that the tide is out.
To what end, in this acoustic age, I write,
I can't be sure. Please say hello to Diane.
Our growing up and learning mark us, but
place is what shapes us and can alter us.
I know I'm not so much myself as I am
the places in which I've lived, live today.
Place is contemplation not less than action,
it helps identify sadness and joy;
it's what we go ahead with, and return to.
Constant as our blue lives can never be,
setting and challenging our values, place
is the unsettled settlement of the mind.
I must learn to recognize this one, and yours;
we cannot live, one without the other.

(1978)

# IV
# WHAT IT WAS

# Dinghies at a Dock

Two & three deep, nudging one another,
squeaking, squealing, creaking,
the gunnel of one riding up over the gunnel of another,
yanking screws, tearing the gunnel fender;
two & three deep, pulling at their painters as the wake
of a passing boat lifts them, quakes
their very dinginess, discombobulates
the pack of them, causing them to smack
one another and generally mash-up,
separating then bringing them back together,
even as wind & tide confuse them, rascals
at bay, the dinghies crowd the dock
waiting purpose, direction
like my dim thoughts first thing each day.

## Swamped

In that position with her decks awash
as if her heart were broken, she has no name
nor class. When did she last hear "Hard-
a-lee!"? What owner would his charge so disclaim?

The jib flies shredded, the main with but one stop.
Rudder, tiller, paddle—these are missing;
bucket, sponge, floor boards, a cap,
and sheets uncoiled are all that's left for stealing.

Small miracle she floats upright at all,
tell-tails streaming, mooring pennant secure,
that vandals have not looted her
or trucked her in the night to Mackinaw.

Isn't it odd that boatyard workers don't care,
that sailors passing, pass by and stare?

# Beetle Cat Race, Labor Day

The wind is sou'west & smoky, say,
or nor'east, gusting & clear;
the tide low & rising, say,
or high & falling.
The course? Say

it starts off White's Flat, goes down
to the bridge & back,
out to the harbor mouth, then up in the marsh,
around an osprey nest, & back
to Bailey's Ridge, around Nun 4,
& then to the finish line off Can 5.

The options? It's about sailing,
of course, & tactics, but is it not mostly
about local knowledge?
On this estuary
wind as much as wind-shadow,
and tide as much as eddy
determine strategy
                      which
is not to mention knowing
the meanders among the marsh
and when to put the centerboard
up or down
or somewhere in-between.

One of the river rats wins,
of course; but say
you did not place last
& nothing went wrong for once
that you couldn't right;
say you had a good sail
& if you did not get the silver,
you got this poem.

## What It Was

A pram, she was some sweet to row
it was good to go between
the dock & boat in her
but you didn't have to be going anywhere
to enjoy her, you could just row
or maneuver her
the better to position her
at the still point between
forward & back
or you could idle
with the oars upraised
their wet blades gleaming in the warm sun

At day's end, you pulled her up
and overturned her on the float
tying the painter to a ring
and when you walked away from her
and saw two red flags flat-out
against the sky lowering
heard their snapping
you knew what it was
you wanted never to lose

## How Like a Painting

How like a painting, she thought looking out
over the anchorage at high tide
bathed in the golden light of late afternoon
and then, as if out of the canvas, she saw
the dinghy rowing in and him in it.
Later, she looked out over the harbor that
had lost its radiant glow and despite the breeze,
cool on her skin, like his fingers tickling,
she knew she hadn't felt like this in ages,
hadn't felt the heat, her flesh stretched taut
as a canvas, its sunset colors rippling,
taking shapes, the shapes unfathomed depth,
the whole transfigured. But would the rower come
again? And would the hour be right? The light?

## Elegy in a Seaside Town

David B. Lawrence, 1916–1986


It was his favorite time of year. He'd worked with the earth
that morning, breathing in its basil and zinnia,
picking its ripe tomatoes, green peppers, cukes, and squash.
To his shop door he smiled, slyly: "Not till Fall!"
and spent the afternoon with old friends sailing,
and went to a charades party after a swordfish dinner.
"I feel the dagger that's been held over me," he said,
referring to heart attacks some years ago, "has lifted."

When he got home, he took the dog out for a walk.
A sou'west wind was blowing and he likely recalled
sailing *Mystery* Down East. She was an Alden yawl.
It was the dog's bark that brought his wife, already in
her best nightgown, outside. He lay there on the lawn,
struck down by lifting winds that left the halyards slapping.

## East of the Bell

We sailed his ashes out
to a bearing he'd plotted east
of the bell. Why here? we wondered.
The ashes were in a can
and each of us tossed a handful
to leeward, over the rail.
They weren't like fireplace ashes—
more like a coarse sand—
and they were heavier than
I'd imagined. We threw
some flowers after them
and watched a bridled tern
swoop down, then climb upwind.
The wind in the rigging seemed
to say nothing and all there was
to say, as the ashes spread

and sank. *Blue Wing* lay
hove-to in waves whitened by
what Dave called "a hatful of wind."
And then she gave us quite
a ride on a close reach back
into the river, her blue
hull heeled, lifting us
over the outgoing tide.
Had we set him free,
on his last sail? Would some-
one do the same for ...
East of the bell was silence.

## Lines on a Dinghy

> For every force there is an equal and opposing force
> —Isaac Newton, Second Law

Any time you step in or out of one,
    thinking you're sure-footed,
it will, having a mind of its own,
    step away, leaving you uprooted.

A dinghy trails behind, a sleeping dog,
    ready when you claim it;
but when, in calm or gale or thick fog,
    it bites the hull, who can blame it?

When you go ashore it stays behind,
    a horse outside a saloon;
but when you come back, late and in a bind,
    it breaks free, neighing "See ya soon!"

In it, with any luck, you're in-between
    the drain and charge of amps,
at ease; but this of course is when,
    in a passing wake, it swamps.

And this says not a word on how to tow
    one or where, on the boat, to stow
what, once out of the water, goes
    from house cat to water buffalo.

Though dangled, dragged, capsized, swamped, and bailed,
    or just sitting pretty;
though motored, rowed, sculled, or sailed,
    it never loses *its* dignity.

And a dinghy, no matter what you do,
    gets the last word—you know:
"Like, without me, Old Friend, where would you
    have gone, be now, or hope to go?"

## Luck of the Strike

One morning, late, while at my desk
    I heard the sirens pass
the Point and cross the bridge to Tripp's
    Boatyard. What is this?

Within the hour word was out:
    Mark and Bruce were dead.
Launching their Hobie Cat, they had
    forgotten overhead

the band of black electric wires.
    Mark and Bruce were fried—
Mark instantly, Bruce inside
    the siren's wailing tires.

They were as competent a pair
    as ever tuned a car
or rig. Mark had run a schooner
    from Maine to Madagascar,

while Bruce had crossed the pond twice,
    once racing. Inside their shop
they tuned my truck, but boats offshore
    had been our common top-

ic. One year later with a boat
    not mine and not a Cat
but on a ramp just up the shore,
    I did the same thing: it sat

astride a trailer, mast stepped and tall,
    the owner's hopes as high,
and down the ramp I backed until—
    *crunch!*—the mast toppled,

broken at the winches, a sound
> heartbreaking. Let's just say
transmitters failed and neurons stalled
> on Westport Point those days.

The difference, that I am here,
> recalling Mark and Bruce?
Their mast was made of some alloy,
> mine of Sitka spruce.

## North Wind Blowing

These pictured walls are home.
They're strong walls and right
for us, but through the open window now comes
a north wind blowing,

a fair departure. What
are we here for?
I regret leaving, that you feel cheated by
the north wind blowing.

This is not easy, you know.
I've done it before,
sworn not to go again—it has its price,
the north wind blowing.

But I cannot stay on land.
Some things I can't
live up to. I cannot stay an old proud fear nor
the north wind blowing.

# V
# MOORING SPARS

## Sailor at a Sawbuck

These are not masts
but trees limbed and felled,
crosscut into twenty-inch logs,
maul-split, and stacked
by the cord into woodpiles
for the beat against winter.
"Back from the islands, Cap?"
a neighbor asks, jocosely,
with no idea that the one
who wields the chainsaw
is the ghost of a sailor,
his position fixed
at the sawbuck; that he's gaining
weight, going nowhere,
stands insensate with the sawdust
and the wind without face
that lifts up and scatters
the spindrift leaf-fall ...
"Dangerous out there, isn't it?"

In from the sawbuck,
the sailor, not hearing
gull cries, sees curling
in a thin drift of smoke
a splash of fire:
and dolphins then,
whales and flying fish,
wind-shifts and squalls,
old friends and new,
gales and the days running
down the distances,
days by design driven ...
In the heat of the logs
the sawbuck sailor
feels again the ocean swell,

sees on the spines
of books surrounding
not the firelight reflected
but the horizon's edge.

# To My Son, Fourteen Months Old, in the Nuclear Age

Hear them? Look! There
go the geese high overhead and honking
in wedges, driving south-by-west,
headed south for winter. They're
flying and making good
time. See them? See them lifting?
What strong wings they have to span the sea
and land in any wind like that!
Hear them

beating? There go the geese,
migrant, wild, shaping
their flight to the shape of the coast,
trailing behind
the Arctic cold. Are you warm enough?
Let me lift you a little higher.
Standing before
these fieldstone walls
and overlooking the water like this,
I sometimes feel
they take us with them up
the glinting tideline road, that we can see
over the round of earth,
behind us

and ahead.
There go the geese. Ask, when you are older,
if in their flight
there isn't something of ours; say
the genius of their instinct holds,
that though the bodies change,
their wedges
fill the flyways.
Point them out shifting and steady,
honking overhead,
coastwise.

# Mishaum Blues

For Frank Lucas

They were countless and thrashing,
a shoal of them churning off the port quarter,
the waters like cottage cheese.
The sou'west wind blew smoky
and the tide—which way was the tide?
In his Whaler, Frank and I were off Mishaum,
showing the boys how to fish:
to fix the lures and cast and jig,
and then to snag the frenzied thing
and play it—*easy, easy*—
and bring it in, boating it with a gaff.
Those we kept we clubbed

and cleaned on the beach (scaling
their iridescence, gutting
their very lives, filleting
the fleshy sides),
and grilled, lightly mayonnaised.
With the blues came fresh corn and zucchini
prepared by our wives, baguettes
and watermelon. Was there ever
a better dinner? A better day?

We're both long divorced.
Our four sons are grown
and no one goes back to Mishaum,
that I know of; but its very name
makes you wonder at the wonder of
the day and how the wonder could
have slipped away, except that it slipped
the way the breeze lets go. Somewhere
I have pictures of us on that windy hill
and someday I'll dig them out.

# The Relic

No one was in the office when I went to ask after
boats like her, which had been built there decades ago,
so I went for a walk around the boatyard,
between Tripp's sheds and behind them,
to the backside of the dunes and it was there I saw her,
abandoned, in the sand and scrub,
like a skeleton surfaced in its grave.

I couldn't believe my luck.
I had come to Westport to meet someone
who'd written about these skiffs,
smaller, recreational versions of work skiffs
used on the river for quahoging and scalloping.
Easy and cheap to build, these 12-footers
were flat-bottomed, with an unstayed cat rig
and leg-o'-mutton sail, and safe as a Schwinn.

"She's yours for the taking," a Tripp said
when finally I found a Tripp,
"else she's bound for the dumpster."
Even as she was, derelict, you could see her sweet sheer,
and how could I let her die in a town dump?
After strapping her together,
I loaded the relic into my pickup and headed home
to the marshlands, creeks, and tidal flats of 'Squam
where the skiff, though too far gone
to restore, would find an afterlife.

You won't want to hear the details about
how I took her measurements, took her apart,
made patterns from her every piece,
then built new strakes, frames, stem, transom ...
Of course I did some things differently—
the fastenings are bronze, not galvanized.

She's a delight to sail, as my kids now know,
besting the channel tide in an eddy, skimming
over the marsh on a falling tide
with the wind astern and a song in her strakes.
Being six feet four and fifty pounds heavier
than the skiff, well ... I take my chances
in something of a different sort.

# Tonging

Everyday at mid-tide with the tips
of marsh grass grazing the hull,
you'd see him out there bellowing
the poles in length twice his height
and longer than the skiff.
And no mean trick, that, to keep
your balance while leaning over the rail
and working those poles, even in
a skiff beamy and flat-bottomed.

Except for the goods in the mud
that once brought up and inboard
filled the bushel baskets and looked,
in any light, bright as silver dollars,
it was like digging fencepost holes,
tonging. He had his favorite spots,
which he'd decoy by working others.

The work made Harry Williams hungry
but not for the work's harvest;
the quahog, if he ate one, gave him hives.
His hunger was for something else.
Like osprey landing on their nests,
Harry was part of the river view
until one day he was nowhere in sight
and the skiff, its prop inlaid in sand
and baskets overturned, lay hard
aground, out on the Lion's Tongue.

Was it not for the solitude
beneath the dome of sky, out
in the weather of it, that he worked
those tongs, withstood the shoulder pain?
Was that how he'd come to accept
the river out of its watershed running,
its tides pulsing in from the sea
against the wind, often enough,
and sweeping out? He never said.

# Gleam, Vanishing Saltmarsh

After Robinson Jeffers


While this saltmarsh, place of renewal, dies because of marina build-up, too many moorings, overfishing and its depletion of predator species
(i.e., while blue crabs decline, allowing purple marsh crabs to thrive and feed on the roots of the cord grass that hold marshes together);

while carbon monoxide thickens, warming the planet, melting ice caps, causing the oceans' rise, acidifying it, now rolling with plastics,
and the weakened peat is overwhelmed by the tide, pulled apart, sucked clean, dissolved, and swept away;

and protest, no matter science, common sense, the essential rightness of conservation, is disregarded, contested, mocked,
I sadly smiling remember that nothing is permanent, neither in nature or man, that the only constant is change.

You doing your thing, doing the degradation: not your fault; life is cool, whether prolonged by medicine or cut short, perhaps mercifully: galaxies beyond ours are not needed less than coral reefs: gleam, vanishing saltmarsh.
But for my children, I would have them not keep their distance from the degradation, rather engage it by reimagining energy's making and use, and the creed for man's survival from dominance of, to harmony with, nature.

And boys, be in nothing so passionate as a love of the environment, on which man totally depends, a vengeful servant, a waking master.
Through this saltmarsh, the most productive of natural resources, turns the tide, which nourishes and can drown and, it is said, return glacially, as ice.

## The Uninsured

Columbus Day has come & gone
& Ishmael is Ichabod again
The harbor hangs on winter's wall
like a cupboard empty except for

the sloop set for a dash to Martinique
the ketch poised for the Panama Canal
a sportfisherman shortly to sprint for the Keys
a schooner not to be left behind

And come Xmas, the New Year
where will they be, the boats
& their owners who can't afford the premiums
or don't believe in them—

which where they were, safe
& which on the beach, frames caved in
& which at sea, lost
& which tied up to a palm tree?

## The Broadbills

In Mystic Seaport's Special Collections,
behind trick walls that, unlocked, open into corridors
of shelves & drawers,
among narwhale tusks & sperm whale teeth,
in a drawer lined in velvet sculpted to hold each one,
lie swordfish bills preserved,
in length one-third their fishes' run,
a few with provenance, each labeled,
all sanded smooth & sharp,
many with wooden hilts attached
to suit man's idea of a proper sword;
others on their convex side oil-painted & lacquered
or in black ink incised,
some with ships half-steam, half-sail;

and carved in relief
on its fibrous elongated upper jaw, beginning there,
one of a mermaid whose tapered tail rises
over ample hips & slender torso
to full breasts & blossom cheeks
                          and, best of all,
to strands of wild hair flowing upward,
their length that of her whole being,
                              bespeaking what
if not the wild sensuality of the fish, its power,
mystical to those of us who hunted it for food,
harpooned it, and dream of it wild still

                                   its bill
designed to slash a school of squid or mackerel,
the easier to go down its toothless mouth;
to counter makos, man,
retaliate for pain inflicted by tooth or iron;
proclaim its whole sleek self, male or female,

a warrior, a ruler of the sea—
even as man's long-line, gill-net, driftnet do
their thoughtful, high-tech best to kill
the stock, usurp the sea's own plan.

## A Waiting Game

Launching the skiff, they could feel the spray, ice-cold,
but they had done it before. All they had
to do was get downriver, to the saltmarsh
near the harbor entrance where the eiders
foraged for mussel and clam. Once grounded on
the marsh, their skiff became a kind of duck blind,
marsh grasses woven onto a folding frame
that rose, shoulder-high, up from the gunnels.
They set up decoys—wooden, hand-painted, proven.
Then it was a waiting game, watching
with ear and eye, and keeping warm enough
and calm to aim and ...
                            Hunting eider is
as good as hunting gets. The worse the weather,
the bleaker the sky, the better for the sea duck,
known for its down and not bad tasting.
It's bitter freezing gales that rouse the birds
and bitter freezing gales that rouse the men,
and these were seasoned hunters, and not only of ducks;
Jack was just back from a Kenyan safari.

Powered by a new electric outboard,
hugging the shore, keeping in the eddy
and out of the freezing spray, downriver they went,
dawn's light dim in heavy clouds behind them.
Wearing camo gear and gloves and waders,
and boasting double-barreled shotguns and brandy,
they wouldn't have wanted much more weight in the skiff—
fifteen feet, aluminum, bluff-bowed
and staunch, with a slight V bottom, molded strakes.

What went wrong as they reached the Lion's Tongue
at the river's bend would be hard to say.
Somebody moved in not quite the right way,
his weight shifting the boat's balance
and the wind lifting his body like a sail, maybe,

as the current shook the boat like a cat
shakes a bird in its mouth, and a wave swamped it,
causing it to capsize. Or did its bow,
caked with ice, not rise on a wave but balk,
turning the boat broadside?
                                    Into the waters,
thick with hammerhead ice floes, the trio fell.
Taken by the tide, the boat took off
up-side-down, untended. The men, all in
their fifties and none in life jackets, shifted
for themselves. One, taller than the others,
walked ashore at Corey's Island. Later,
he was lifted clear by helicopter.

As the boat, whose engine shaft had hung up on
a weir, was hauled out of the river's reach
that afternoon, and the mourning gathered momentum—
the bodies of the others had washed up
at the turn of the tide inside the entrance jetty—
and TV journalists pressed for a lead story
(there was no suspicion of wrong-doing)
and Dave Duval, in hospital suffering
hypothermia, tried to think things through
(Why had *he* survived?), a flock of eiders rose up
from the mussel beds and flew like the Blue Angels
in a kind of salute, to windward, above the tide.

## Under Poncho

It was the winter of '77,
    in January no doubt.
The river's eastern branch stood frozen,
    the boisterous wind was out

of the north. We rigged a surplus poncho
    over a wooden frame,
and drove up Drift Road to Hix Bridge,
    and launched our makeshift claim

to fame. Holding shoulder-high
    the sail's cross-beam, we headed south
on skates and hoped to reach the bridge,
    if not the harbor mouth.

The channel was not a main concern
    and neither, for once, was the tide.
There were no stripers or blues to catch;
    eiders flew safe on glide.

Past islands great and small we cruised,
    and down through marsh blades west
of Speaking Rock and Little Ram.
    Although the cruise seemed blessed,

we often tacked to dodge a rock
    or clump of frozen grass.
Off Masquesatch, the ice turned slush
    and I fell on my ass.

After changing skates for boots
    upon the western shore,
we toasted the North Wind with rum
    and walked to Bobby's car.

The sail? Into the freezing air
    we let it have its run
to zig and zag, higher and higher,
    beneath the winter sun.

And though there's been no skating since,
    the poncho soars in gusts
as if a kite whose string, even
    as we pull it, pulls us.

## Elegy Sketched in an Estuary Cove

Christopher R. Gillespie, 1942–2015

Last night, a cold January night
on the coast, a friend who loved nothing better
than a sail on a summer day, died in bed.
As well as anyone, he understood
the estuary tide and eddies, knew
the channel curves and rocks, the salt marsh creeks,
the sound and pull of cord grass grazing the hull,
and where in peat to find the choicest quahogs.
He won his share of races, and lost them too.
Summer nights, in the moonlight, he'd anchor out
for a picnic alone with his wife (the no-see-ums
notwithstanding), other nights with their kids and friends.
It was the west branch of the river he knew best.
He'd sketch it time and again, in different media,
knowing he would never sketch what he saw,
how he knew it, its pulse his own.

This morning the river is frozen over in
its upper reaches, ragged with ice floes at
the harbor mouth where waves, white-maned, break.
You wouldn't think in a time like this a man
like him would have his boat in the water,
out in the cove, that he'd row out to her,
raise the sail, and let go the mooring.
But it's not what you think about—cancer.
Surely in his mind, in his dream of life,
the boat heeled and hummed as she surged ahead
on the boisterous sou'west wind, a bone in her teeth,
eliciting his balance, his windward stance.

# Arrival, Westport Point

We were in a sloop, chartered out of Hadley's,
and had beat from Robinson's Hole across Buzzards Bay
under reefed main and jib
in a twenty-knot sou'west breeze
against an incoming tide that day.

Watching the tower fall off to port,
we did not make Gooseberry Neck
and had to beat back out, past
the Hen and Chickens, into the Sound.
Making the tack,
the jib sheet block
jammed on the traveller and, freeing it,
the club boom whacked my head.
                                        Finally,
a bearing gave us the tack toward land.
With, in the offshore view,
Horseneck and Acoaxet beaches overlapping,
you cannot see the harbor entrance hiding
between them; but a bell buoy,
soundings, and a spindle showed the way,
and with eased sheets we entered the estuary.

It was to see an old classmate I'd come. Passing
The Knubble and boathouse row,
we saw suddenly the view
upriver and east to the Point, its roofs
and lawns sloping down to the town wharf
and the fishboats moored there
and yachts on moorings.
To two accustomed to asphalt shimmering
like a mirage with traffic's carbon monoxide,
the saltmarsh, golden, seemed an open range,
its creeks and shores, its tides inviting.
Where land meets river, and river the sea,
here was an anchorage, a place of exchange.

## Mooring Spars

Oak or pine and six feet long,
four-by-four inches square,
pressure-treated, through-bolted hung,
replacing summer's plastic spheres,

spars mark the moorings—radiators
or engine blocks, mushroom anchors,
bathtubs and coffins filled with cement,
anything but what's apparent.

Heavy chain connects them, nothing
ice or hunger or a grudge
could cut, saw, gnaw, or budge.
Barnacles to their links are clinging.

Athwart the wind, against the tide
that toys with them, they ride, they ride.

# Acknowledgements

*Anthology of South Shore Poets:* East of the Bell; Elegy in a Seaside Town
*The Boston Monthly:* Letter from Westport Point
*The Country Journal:* Requiem for a Shrimp Boat
*Gloucester:* Outside the Steamer Lanes
*Harvard Magazine:* Andy's, in Winter
*Light:* Lines on a Dinghy
*Poetry:* China Royal Restaurant; Fog; Wind Against the Tide
*Poetry Porch:* Capsized; Dinghies at a Dock; Mooring Spars; Paddling Home; The Relic; Swamped; The Uninsured; What It Was
*Sail:* At Anchor; In an Eddy; In a Shed; The Launching; North Wind Blowing; Taking out the Mooring
*Sailing:* On Her Mooring
*West Crook Review:* The Loss of the *Navigator;* Sailor at a Sawbuck

❦

Cover photo by Richard Dey
Author photo by Alex Dey

❦

Thanks to everyone who has had a hand in shaping these poems over the years. "The Relic" is an imaginary reconstruction based on the article "Rebirth of a Westport Pond Boat," by Tim Sullivan, which appeared in *WoodenBoat* No. 242. "A Waiting Game" is an imaginary reconstruction of a similar event that was widely reported in the media in January 2014.

RICHARD DEY studied with Elizabeth Bishop and Robert Fitzgerald at Harvard College, and was poetry editor of *The Harvard Advocate*. He had previously attended a writers' conference featuring James Dickey, and served in the U.S. Army as a journalist. A graduate of Tabor Academy where he sailed in the schooner *Tabor Boy*, he has worked as a commercial fisherman, yacht skipper, freelance journalist, editor, and as a professor of maritime history and literature in a college program along the Atlantic seaboard and Lesser Antilles. He is included on the Williams College-Mystic Seaport website for Searchable Sea Literature, https://sites.williams.edu/searchablesealit/.

Printed in the United States
By Bookmasters